Then and Now

Contents

Life long ago 2

Homes 4

Clothes 6

Food 8

Travel 10

School 12

Playtime 14

Index 16

Life long ago

Life was very different about 150 years ago.
There were no cars, buses or aeroplanes.

Homes and clothes were also very different. What if you had lived long ago? How would your life have been different?

Homes then

People had to get water from a pump in the street. The toilet was outside the house.

Homes now

Water comes into the kitchen and bathroom through pipes.

Clothes then

Most clothes were made by hand. Girls wore skirts and long dresses. Only boys wore trousers.

Clothes now

Most clothes are made in factories. Girls can wear trousers, skirts and dresses.

Food then

People went to small shops every day. It was hard to keep food fresh.

Food now

People go to the supermarket about once a week. Fridges keep food fresh for longer.

Travel then

People did not travel very far. Horses pulled coaches and trams. They went very slowly.

Travel now

People can travel a long way. Cars, buses, trains and aeroplanes all go very fast.

School then

One teacher taught all the classes together in one room. There were not many books to read.

School now

Most schools have many classrooms. Each class has a different teacher. There are lots of books to read.

Playtime then

Children played games with marbles. They also played hide-and-seek.

Playtime now

Children play games on computers, but they still enjoy hide-and-seek!

Index

aeroplanes 2, 11

books 12, 13

buses 2, 11

cars 2, 11

computers 15

factories 7

games 14, 15

horses 10

school 12, 13

shops 8

teacher 12, 13

toilet 4

water 4, 5